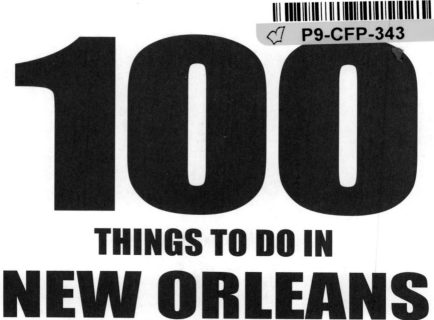

100

THINGS TO DO IN

NEW ORLEANS

BEFORE YOU

DIE

THINGS TO DO IN
NEW ORLEANS
BEFORE YOU
DIE

BETH D'ADDONO

Library of Congress Control Number: 2016940404

ISBN: 9781681060583

Cover Image: Pat Garin

Design by Jill Halpin

Printed in the United States of America
16 17 18 19 20   5 4 3 2 1

Please note that websites, phone numbers, addresses, and company names are subject to change or cancellation. We did our best to relay the most accurate information available, but due to circumstances beyond our control, please do not hold us liable for misinformation. When exploring new destinations, please do your homework before you go.

DEDICATION

For my dear friend Sammye Levy,
who made New Orleans feel like home from the start.

For the people of New Orleans who have welcomed me with open
hearts and arms, my life is so much better because of you.

• •

CONTENTS

● ●

Music and Entertainment

Sports and Recreation

Culture and History

• •

Shopping and Fashion

• •

PREFACE

Have you ever been to a place that felt like home from the moment you arrived?

In this place, you immediately feel comfortable in your own skin. An openness blooms in your heart, and somehow you are drawn to kindred spirits who share your passion. This point on the map spurs you in mysterious ways—to be better, do better, imagine more for yourself—and when you leave this same geographic dot, you are overcome with a mournful longing that can only be assuaged by returning to the source of your addiction.

For me, that place is New Orleans.

From the first time I visited in 1991 to write a story for a magazine, it became my obsession. My visits and assignments became more frequent, often to write about the city, but sometimes just to satisfy my craving. Over time, the connection I felt for New Orleans grew stronger. Like a lover who refuses to be ignored, the Crescent City's siren call became insistent.

I finally listened to my heart and moved here in 2012—first to a cozy little apartment in the Marigny, within walking distance of everything I loved, and now I live in the 7th Ward on a street with deep neighborhood roots and a strong sense of pride and community. I have so much still to learn about New Orleans and a lifetime in which to do it.

• •

Narrowing my picks to just 100 things was a tough one, especially because with its haunted past, New Orleans will likely have things for you to do after you die, but this lineup is a good start. So many of my favorite places and flavors and experiences are on these pages. I hope you have as much fun discovering New Orleans as I continue to have every day.

A special thanks to all the locals who continue to generously share their experiences with me. I'm also grateful to the hardworking PR teams at the New Orleans CVB and New Orleans Tourism Marketing Corporation. Thank you all for your expertise and support.

• •

Photo Credit: LouisianaNorthshore.com

FOOD AND DRINK

CELEBRATE A MILESTONE
AT RESTAURANT AUGUST

While you can't go wrong with a table at any of chef John Besh's dozen eateries, if you're trying to impress or need to be feted in style, reserve a table at Restaurant August, a swank special occasion spot in the Central Business District. From the nineteenth-century French-Creole setting to white-glove service and impeccable Gulf-to-table cuisine, August never disappoints. The kitchen's fried green tomatoes topped with lobster, shrimp, and tangy remoulade raise this Southern classic to lofty heights. If you're feeling flush, order the chef's tasting with paired wine—expensive but unforgettable. If you're wining and dining a vegetarian, the Farmers Market menu is an elegant option with such dishes as slow-cooked butternut squash with shaved truffle, smoked onion, and wild mushrooms.

301 Tchoupitoulas St., 504-299-9777
restaurantaugust.com

Other restaurants guaranteed to impress:

Emeril's Delmonico
1300 St. Charles Ave.,
504-525-4937
emerilsrestaurants.com/emerils-delmonico

Le Petit Grocery
4238 Magazine St.,
504-891-3377
http://www.lapetitegrocery.com

The Grill Room at Windsor Court
300 Gravier St.,
504-522-1994
grillroomneworleans.com

Broussard's
819 Conti St.,
504-581-3866
broussards.com

EAT FLAMING BANANAS FOSTER
AT BRENNAN'S

Brennan's, the storied restaurant that has anchored Creole dining on Royal Street since 1946, was treated to a stunning $20 million redo in 2014, but thankfully some things didn't change. Restaurateur Ralph Brennan and partner Terry White knew that there was no messing with the bananas foster, a flaming orgy of bananas, butter, and rum-fueled goodness invented by Owen Brennan in the early 1950s. The cinnamon-scented spectacle is the perfect ending to chef Slade Rushing's creative take on Brennan's cuisine, including eggs Sardou, roasted oysters with smoked chili butter, and mahi mahi amandine. And, yes, you can have dessert at breakfast, the eye-opening indulgence served at Brennan's from 9 a.m. during the week and 8 a.m. on the weekend.

417 Royal St., 504-525-9711
brennansneworleans.com

SLURP SOME BAM!
BBQ SHRIMP
AT EMERIL'S

To the rest of the world, Emeril Lagasse is a celebrity chef, cookbook author, and creator of a line of specialty seasonings. To New Orleanians, he's our Chef Emeril, the guy who wowed at Commander's and then opened his flagship Emeril's Restaurant in the Warehouse District in 1990, long before the neighborhood became fashionable. Emeril's, now under the watch of chef de cuisine David Slater, remains sharply focused. The barbecue shrimp is one dish that will never leave the menu, a spicy, peppery simmer of Gulf shrimp in Worcestershire, butter, wine, and hot sauce that is still the gold standard for this local fave. Deliciously sloppy to slurp, best mopped up with a crusty pistolette, Emeril's barbecue shrimp is the bomb.

800 Tchoupitoulas St., 504-528-9393
emerilsrestaurants.com

MANGIA SWEETS SICILIAN STYLE
AT ANGELO BROCATO

Angelo Brocato, a family business that has dished silky gelato and traditional Italian sweets since the turn of the last century, is a Mid-City icon. Steeped in old-world charm, this is the place for anise biscotti, espresso-laced tiramisu, or house-made cassata cake. The gelato is the stuff of dreams, studded with pistachio, shot through with caramel, oozing dark chocolate. Then there's the granita—Italian ice bright with such fruit as local satsumas and watermelon, the perfect way to chill on a hot summer's day. Shapely Italian beauties smile behind the counter, expertly piping ricotta to order into cannoli shells. Pair with a dark espresso from the shiny copper machine and all is right with the world.

214 N. Carrollton Ave., 504-486-0078
angelobrocatoicecream.com

DEVOUR A COCHON DE LAIT PO-BOY
AT KATIE'S

If you're a fan of the addictive cochon de lait po-boy revered at Jazz Fest but don't often find yourself at the most excellent Walker's Barbecue in New Orleans East, chef Scot Craig can help. Craig is chef/owner at Katie's Restaurant in Mid-City, a much-loved neighborhood Creole-Italian eatery that draws armies of regulars for lunch, brunch, and dinner. Craig's version of the slow-roasted suckling pig is off the hook, tender shards of swiney goodness piled high on a buttered, lightly toasted Gendusa roll smothered with Creole mustard-tanged slaw. The sandwich, like everything at Katie's, is oversized and swoonworthy. What a treat to dine at a restaurant that always exceeds expectations, whether dishing a humble po-boy, fried Gulf seafood, or a slab of Debbie Does Doberge cake for dessert.

Katie's Restaurant
701 Iberville St., 504-488-6582
katiesinmidcity.com

Walker's Barbecue
10828 Hayne Blvd., 504-241-8227
cochondelaitpoboys.com

SNAP TO JAZZ BRUNCH
AT COMMANDER'S PALACE

Sunday jazz brunch is a New Orleans tradition, and there's no better place to have it than Commander's Palace. The very sight of the green-and-white awning is enough to get the stomach rumbling. Visitors may hail the circa 1880 Garden District grand dame, but it's fiercely beloved by locals. Both Emeril Lagasse and Paul Prudhomme started here, and the Brennan family has maintained a tradition of culinary excellence since 1969. Chef Tory McPhail, a James Beard award winner, keeps the menu relevant and the emphasis squarely on local product, seafood, and game. Commander's weekend jazz brunch is pricey but epic, with such choices as turtle soup, blue crab frittata, and one of the best bread puddings in town.

1403 Washington Ave., 504-899-8221
commanderspalace.com

More jazz brunches to try:

Atchafalaya
901 Louisiana Ave.,
504-891-9626
atchafalayarestaurant.com

Mr. B's Bistro
201 Royal St.,
504 523-2078
mrbsbistro.com

Court of Two Sisters
613 Royal St.,
courtoftwosisters.com

Buffa's Bar & Restaurant
1001 Esplanade Ave.,
504-949-0038
buffasbar.com

REVIVE YOUR CORPSE
AT THE COCKTAIL BAR

New Orleans debauchery can take its toll. If your hung-over corpse needs reviving, head to the Cocktail Bar at the lobby in the posh Windsor Court in the CBD, an oasis of sanity in a city where excess is the baseline. Seasoned mixologist Kent Westmoreland counts the enervating Corpse Reviver No. 2 in his top five overall cocktails thanks to its exquisite balance of gin, Cointreau, Lillet blanc, citrus, and dash of absinthe. Popularized in the 1930 *Savoy Cocktail Book* by Harry Craddock, think of this classic cocktail as a lemon drop with a Ph.D. Served up very cold in a fetching coup glass, its effect is dangerously bracing.

300 Gravier St., 504-523-6000
windsorcourthotel.com

EAT BEIGNETS
BY THE RIVER

An all-time favorite New Orleans experience is to order takeaway beignets from Cafe du Monde and commandeer a bench facing the Mississippi. Wander that way just about any time and you'll see folks with the same idea, clouds of powdered sugar swirling in the air like gnats on an August eve. These deep-fried pillows of dough, served round the clock at the open air original Cafe du Monde on Decatur, come three to an order, hot from the fryer, and dusted with powdered sugar, best enjoyed with chicory-laced café au lait on the side. Adored by locals and visitors alike, beignets are a treat any time of day, a possibility since Cafe du Monde is open 24 hours a day, seven days a week.

800 Decatur St., 504-525-4544
cafedumonde.com

SUCK THE HEADS
AT FRANKIE & JOHNNY'S

March through June is crawfish season in New Orleans, an annual happening that is met with an anticipation usually reserved for Mardi Gras in neighborhoods and restaurants all over town. Seafood take-out corner stores offer crawfish spiced and boiled by the pound, and local bars simmer the popular mudbugs on rotating nights of the week. Frankie & Johnny's, Uptown, is a popular place to eat the spicy treat, a neighborhood joint with a friendly local crowd and reasonable prices. The number one way to eat crawfish is out of a traditional boil, with potatoes, smoked sausage and corn, and plenty of napkins—and you're a local or can pass as one if you suck the flavorful juices out of the crawfish head (and body). Too much trouble? Order the etouffee.

321 Arabella St., 504-243-1234
frankieandjohnnys.net

Four more places to eat mudbugs:

Cooter Brown's
509 S. Carrollton Ave.,
504-866-9104
cooterbrowns.com

Cosimo's
1201 Burgundy St.,
504-522-9715

Mid-City Yacht Club
440 S. Saint Patrick St.,
504-483-2517
midcityyachtclub.com

R Bar
1431 Royal St.,
504-9949-7499
royalstreetinn.com

EAT STEAK FAMILY STYLE
AT CRESCENT CITY

New Orleanians love their beef. After all, this is the city where the diminutive powerhouse Ruth Fertel founded Ruth's Chris Steak House in 1965, now a megachain with locations worldwide. For many locals, though, the bacon-wrapped filet sizzled in butter at Crescent City Steaks is the gold standard. Founded by Croatian immigrant John Vojkovich in 1934, the still family-owned restaurant was the first to serve slabs of prime aged beef in New Orleans. But beyond the fair prices, comfortable setting, and stellar steakhouse fare, Crescent City oozes the particular brand of hospitality that is the calling card of a true New Orleans institution. Servers treat regulars like family, but unlike a few entrenched neighborhood restaurants where outsiders may feel they've wandered into a private club, Crescent City's welcome mat is for all.

1001 N. Broad St., 504-821-3271
crescentcitysteaks.com

DIVE INTO A SLICE
OF DOBERGE

A six-layer doberge cake turns any day into a special occasion. Doberge is a favorite in New Orleans, a treat created by Beulah Ledner in the 1930s as a lighter version of Hungarian dobos torta, with pudding replacing buttercream filling. She Frenchified the name to doberge (say dough-bash), and a classic was born. Besides Gambino's, the Metairie bakery that acquired the name and recipe in 1946, Debbie Does Doberge in the Warehouse District bakes an ethereal torte in various flavors, such as salted caramel, red velvet, and peanutbutterscotch. Her storefront Bakery Bar is a cozy bar with nibbles in case you want to pair your slice with a drink. By the way, Debbie is actually Charlotte McGehee and Charles Mary IV, but they figured Debbie Does Doberge is harder to forget.

1179 Annunciation St., 504-616-2330
debbiedoesdoberge.com

TIP
You can also order slices of DDD
at Katie's Restaurant and Toup's Meatery.

Katie's Restaurant, 3701 Iberville St., 504-488-6582
katiesinmidcity.com

Toup's Meatery, 845 N. Carrollton Ave., 504-252-4999
toupsmeatery.com

SIP A FRENCH 75
AT FRENCH 75 BAR

Named after a 75-millimeter field gun used in World War I, the French 75 is a bubbly wonder that elegantly hits its mark every time. The best place to have one is at Arnaud's French 75 Bar, originally a "gentlemen only area" when Frenchman Arnaud Cazenav founded Arnaud's in 1918. Now the purview of legendary local barman Chris Hannah, French 75 is a cocktail and cigar lounge that makes you feel grown up, even if you aren't. Although some recipes for this sparkler are made with gin, Hannah always uses cognac. In case you were wondering, he also makes a perfect Sazerac. Trust him, he'll never steer you wrong. Have lunch or dinner at Arnaud's for a taste of renowned Creole cuisine.

813 Bienville, 504-523-5433
arnaudsrestaurant.com/bars/french-75/

TIP

While you're at Arnaud's, extend the festive mood with a visit to the Germaine Cazenave Wells Mardi Gras Museum upstairs, a lavish costume display that will have you longing for Carnival season.

GADABOUT OVER FRIDAY LUNCH
AT GALATOIRE'S

Friday lunch is a locals' tradition at Galatoire's on Bourbon Street, a big-time notable for high fashion, flowing champagne, and decadent excess. New Orleanians dressed to impress line up early for the 11:30 seating or more likely pay a "sitter" to wait in line for them. Reservations aren't taken for Friday lunch, and with only 41 tables and 132 seats in the coveted first-floor dining room, competition is fierce. But snag a table and you'll see a convivial scene of table-hopping, martini drinking, hoots of laughter, and the occasional outbreak of song. Lunch is endless, usually still loudly carrying on come dinnertime. Through it all, the best waiters in the city serve platters of trout meuniere, shrimp remoulade, and stuffed eggplant, a tradition that hopefully will never change.

209 Bourbon St., 504-525-2021
galatoires.com

**Can't get into Friday lunch at Galatoire's?
Here are four alternatives:**

Restaurant August
301 Tchoupitoulas St., 504-299-9777
restaurantaugust.com

Antoine's
713 St. Louis St., 504-581-4422
antoines.com

Dooky Chase
2301 Orleans Ave., 504-821-0535
dookychaserestaurant.com

Clancy's
6100 Annunciation St., 504-895-1111
clancysneworleans.com

CHILL WITH
A FROZEN DAIQUIRI OR TWO

If you're over 21, the only antidote to New Orleans in August is the frozen daiquiri. First slurped in the small Cuban town of Daiquiri in 1898, the adult version of the sno-ball comes in myriad flavors and Technicolor hues. Walk-up windows are available for ordering the potent refresher all over town, and drive-through daiquiri shacks are also particular to the New Orleans landscape. Even when the temperature is 90° with 90 percent humidity, a frozen margarita daiquiri from New Orleans Original Daiquiris/Fat Tuesdays will set your teeth to chattering. Because this is New Orleans, the daiquiri also has its own fete, September's month-long Daiquiri season, with thirty days of daiquiri tours, special events, and tastings all around town.

18+ New Orleans–area locations
fattuesday.com

GUZZLE A GRASSHOPPER
AT TUJAGUE'S

Equal parts green crème de menthe, white crème de cacao, and heavy cream, a grasshopper is shaken with ice and strained into a chilled cocktail glass, an after-dinner Southern throwback that oozes retro charm. Philip Guichet first created the minty dreamsicle at Tujague's, America's oldest stand up bar, in 1856. The neon green sipper is still a Tujague's signature, served shaken and poured into a champagne flute with a brandy float on top. What better way to drink your dessert than with a revelatory sip at the very bar where it was invented? While you're at it, order a whiskey punch. It was invented here too.

823 Decatur St., 504-525-8676
tujaguesrestaurant.com

TUCK INTO
A BOWL OF GUMBO
AT DOOKY CHASE

Gumbo is a hotly contested specialty in New Orleans, with the best version usually made by your mama. And while arguing over which roux is darker and who serves the best gumbo can be fighting words, mention Dooky Chase and heads start nodding. Often called the Queen of Creole Cuisine, chef/owner Leah Chase has served gumbo to luminaries from Duke Ellington to President Barack Obama, who earned demerits for adding hot sauce to the bowl. Chase's Creole gumbo is just about perfect, swimming with creatures of land and sea, crab, shrimp, and oysters passing time with chicken, sausage, smoked ham, and veal brisket. Her roux is rich but not too, the flavors spicy but not hot. No wonder this down-home restaurant has been a Treme landmark since 1941.

2301 Orleans Ave., 504-821-0535
dookychaserestaurant.com

More great gumbo:

Mr. B's Bistro
201 Royal St., 504-523-2078
mrbsbistro.com

Casamento's
4330 Magazine St., 504-895-9761
casamentosrestaurant.com

L'il Dizzy's Café
1500 Esplanade Ave., 504-569-8997
lildizzyscafe.net

Gumbo Shop
630 St. Peter St., 504-525-1486
gumboshop.com

ORDER A SNO-BALL
FROM HANSEN'S SNO-BLIZ

New Orleans sno-balls are to sno-cones what Degas is to paint by number ballerinas. No mere flavoring of crudely crushed ice, sno-balls are more like the shave ice popular in Hawaii. It was Ernest and Mary Hansen who pioneered the treat with Ernest's patented Sno-Bliz ice machine back in 1939. Mary dreamed up endless flavors made from simple syrups, fruit, and condensed milk or whipped cream. Now in the hands of granddaughter Ashley, the stand is a hallmark of imaginative combinations and superior quality perfected by three generations. The sno-balls at Hansen's drip with handmade syrups in such flavors as ginger and cardamom or the popular Brown Pelican, a cream of root beer that will chill you to the bone. The James Beard Foundation named Hansen's an America's Classic in 2014.

4801 Tchoupitoulas St., 504-891-9788
snobliz.com

THROW BACK A HURRICANE
AT PAT O'S

Hurricanes may be the patron saint of booze along Bourbon Street, but Pat O'Brien's signature drink has a rightful place in New Orleans history. The potent mash-up of passion fruit, citrus, grenadine, and rum was first poured in the 1940s, an alcoholic testimony to human ingenuity. Like many American bars, Pat O'Brien's faced a whiskey shortage after World War II, but there was plenty of cheap rum. After some experimenting, head bartender Louis Culligan had a stroke of brilliance: blend rum with passion fruit mix and serve it in a tall glass shaped like a hurricane lamp, a concoction that is also right at home at retro tiki bars. If you've never sung along to the dueling pianos at Pat O's, hurricane in hand, what are you waiting for?

718 St. Peter St., 504-525-4823
patobriens.com

TIP
Lafitte's on the quieter side of Bourbon
is a tie for the best hurricane in town.

941 Bourbon St., 504-593-9761
lafittesblacksmithshop.com

LINE UP FOR A BLOODY MARY
AT LIUZZA'S ON THE WAY TO FEST

Come Jazz Fest, the streets around the Fair Grounds are choked with brightly plumed fest-goers gleefully greeting pals they haven't seen since last year this time. While all the pubs in the neighborhood are busy, Liuzza's by the Track is ground zero, a mob scene of blissed-out festers whose tradition is to order a spicy Bloody Mary from the bar and slurp it on the way to the track. Packed with veggies, such as pickled beans and okra, this perfect Bloody gives the illusion of being good for you, even if you order a double. When it's not so busy, circle back to this corner bar for a bowl of outstanding gumbo, although the Worcestershire-fueled barbecue shrimp po-boy slathered between a hot pistolette is equally irresistible.

1518 N. Lopez, 504-218-7888
liuzzasnola.com

CROSS THE RIVER FOR CHICKEN A LA GRANDE
AT MOSCA'S

There are a handful of excellent reasons to cross the (thankfully widened) Huey P. Long Bridge to the West Bank. At the top of the list is Mosca's (say MOE-scuz), an esteemed family-run Creole Italian roadhouse that sits along a dark stretch of Highway 90 West. Opened for business in 1946, the restaurant's storied history includes ties to the late Carlos Marcello, a New Orleans crime boss who also happened to be the landlord and a regular. Whatever his issues, the guy had good taste in food. The unchanged menu includes garlic-infused specialties, such as barbecued shrimp, baked oysters, and, of course, the Chicken a la Grande, roasted with tons of fresh garlic, herbs, and white wine. Sounds simple, right? You try making it at home. Mosca's is always better.

4137 U.S. Highway 90 West, Westwego, 504-436-8950
moscasrestaurant.com

SCARF A MUFFALETTA
AT CENTRAL GROCERY

New York has its sub and Philly its overstuffed hoagie. In New Orleans, the only Italian sandwich worth discussing is the muffaletta, an ethereal combination of cured meats, such as ham, mortadella, salami, and cheeses, including provolone and sometimes mozzarella, piled into a (usually) round seeded loaf and dressed with a piquant olive salad. Central Grocery across from the French Market invented the sandwich in 1906 and still has its family flag planted on one of the best versions in town, a monster of a sandwich perfect for sharing. You might have to wait in line, but it's worth it. If you want to sit down and eat, order to go. Central Grocery only has a standing counter for munching.

923 Decatur St., 504-523-1620
centralgrocerynola.com

Four more to try:

Cochon Butcher
930 Tchoupitoulas St., 504-588-7675
cochonbutcher.com

Napoleon House
500 Chartres St., 504-524-9752
napoleonhouse.com

Katie's
3701 Iberville St., 504-488-6582
katiesinmidcity.com

Frank's
933 Decatur St., 504-525-1602

STUMBLE UPON
NONCHALANTLY CHIC N7

You can't make reservations at N7, the hidden gem of a French restaurant in the upper 9th ward, simply because the eatery doesn't have a phone. It also doesn't offer live music, Creole cuisine or New Orleans–inspired décor. What you will find at this unassuming bistro tucked behind a wooden fence just off of St. Claude is a gorgeous, candlelit courtyard; cool French pop music; bistro fare, such as steak au poivre and mussels, along with mostly imported seafood in a can—think smoked sardines and spiced calamari. The wine list is good. Named for the roadway that goes between Paris and the Italian border, N7 used to be a tire shop. Now the only thing you can change there is your attitude.

1117 Montegut St.

CHANNEL YOUR INNER OENOPHILE
AT NOWFE

In a city known for its showstopping gastronomy, the annual New Orleans Wine & Food Experience (NOWFE) shows the penultimate in good taste. Happening annually over Memorial Day weekend, NOWFE delivers the goods with pairing seminars, Q&As with top chefs, and serious sipping. Track trends, rub shoulders with winemakers, explore world viticulture, and get a dose of local color with the help of homegrown music, dozens of chefs, and more than a thousand vintages. Typically attracting some ten thousand gourmands, NOWFE offers indulgence guilt free: the event has raised more than $1 million for local nonprofits since it was founded in 1992. Although the grand finale gala is quite posh, the Royal Street Stroll, an open house of shops and galleries with tastings and nibbles on the street, is a locals' fave.

504-934-1474
nowfe.com

SHUCKS!
SAMPLE OYSTERS RAW
AND CHARBROILED
AT DRAGO'S

The genius notion, to add butter and garlic to a raw oyster's natural brine, using the shell as a ready-made serving dish straight from the grill, is nothing short of brilliant. It occurred to Tommy Cvitanovich a couple of decades ago at Drago's, his family's revered oyster palace on the edge of the French Quarter. Opened by Drago and Klara Cvitanovich in 1969, Drago's makes some of the best charbroiled (some folks say chargrilled) oysters you'll ever taste—juicy, topped with herbs and a blend of Romano and parmesan cheese, sizzling with butter. Drago's has locations in suburban Metairie and Jackson, Mississippi, but the Hilton spot is always a raucous scene, a lively mix of conventioneers and locals getting their fill of raw Gulf beauties or slurping charbroiled, butter dripping down their chins.

Hilton New Orleans Riverside, 2 Poydras St., 504-584-3911
dragosrestaurant.com

TIP

Acme Oyster is another bivalve landmark, regularly shucking more than three million oysters per year, best appreciated from a seat at the scarred marble oyster bar.

724 Iberville St., 504-522-5973
acmeoyster.com

LOOK A FISH IN THE EYE
AT PECHE

With the same unflinching focus they apply to piggy goodness at Cochon, chef/owners Donald Link and Stephen Stryjewski troll for seafood at Peche, an industrial chic eatery in the Warehouse District. This place is all about local and line-caught seafood, most of it cooked on a hardwood fire grill. Chef/partner Ryan Prewitt, who was named Best Chef: South by the James Beard Foundation, delivers intriguing dishes, such as spicy Asian-flavored capellini with crab and chilies and one of the best grilled whole redfish you'll ever eat, a rustic beauty flavored with an herbaceous salsa verde bright with citrus. Save room for pastry chef Maggie Scales's salted peanut pie with chocolate sauce. The menu, the same for lunch and dinner, changes frequently, so reserve early and often.

800 Magazine St., 504-522-1744
pecherestaurant.com

DEVOUR A MESSY ROAST BEEF PO-BOY
AT PARKWAY

Parkway Bakery has defined po-boys in New Orleans for the better part of a century. Folks line up early for the juicy roast beef po-boy, a four-napkiner always ordered "dressed"—with lettuce, tomato, mayonnaise, and pickles. A landmark for rib-sticking eats since 1911, the story goes that Parkway is where the "poor boy" sandwich was invented to feed the round-the-clock workers at the nearby American Can Company when it was still in business. Another tale has the owners of Martin Brothers Coffee Stand sending hearty sandwiches to the city's striking streetcar operators (aka "poor boys"). Doesn't matter—the bottom line is that the sandwiches are delish. Thank goodness neighbor Jay Nix reopened the place in 2003 after a decade of darkness when the original owners closed up shop.

538 Hagan Ave., 504-482-3047
parkwaypoorboys.com

Four more to try:
Killer PoBoys, 219 Dauphine St., 504-462-2731 killerpoboys.com
Liuzza's Restaurant & Bar, 3636 Bienville St., 504-482-9120 liuzzas.com
Domelise's, 5240 Annunciation St., 504-899-9126 domilisespoboys.com
Trenasse, 444 St. Charles Ave., 504-680-7000 trenasse.com

SCALE THE MILE HIGH PIE
IN THE CARIBBEAN ROOM

Time traveling is alive and well in the Caribbean Room, the reopened culinary chestnut in the legendary Pontchartrain Hotel on St. Charles Avenue. The revamp of the grand, jacket-required Caribbean Room, with its Mad Men '60s vibe that once hosted Frank Sinatra and Rita Hayworth, is part of a $10 million overhaul of the Garden District landmark. Chef Chris Lusk and team have resurrected such classic dishes as crab Remick and the famed Mile High Pie and given a contemporary spin to other favorites, such as rabbit and dumplings and red snapper. The restaurant swims against the trendy tide with its palm fronds and white tablecloths, a refreshing throwback that makes dining here a real experience. After dinner, have a drink at the rooftop bar for the best view in town.

2031 St. Charles Ave., 504-323-1500
thepontchartrainhotel.com/food-drink/

SATISFY YOUR
CAVEMAN CARNIVORE
AT PORT OF CALL

Situated on the edge of the Quarter on Esplanade at Dauphine, Port of Call is known for its huge chargrilled burgers and loaded baked potatoes. There are other menu options, chargrilled rib eye, for instance, but that's not why fans line up and wait for a table. At this divey spot, where the décor is faux nautical in thankfully dim lighting, it's all about the burgers and the spuds. One order is easily enough for two people; if you're hungry, add an extra potato and you're still getting off cheap. Now as popular with visitors as with locals, the line is often out the door and the go-cups are a-flowing. Speaking of drinks, the Monsoon is Port of Call's version of the hurricane and beyond potent.

838 Esplanade Ave., 504-523-0120
portofcallnola.com

GET A RAMOS GIN FIZZ MUSTACHE
AT BOURBON O BAR

For the frothiest Ramos Gin Fizz, a favorite of notorious past governor Huey P. Long, go directly to Bourbon O Bar in the Bourbon Orleans Hotel, a stylish den of craft libations with live jazz most evenings. Bartender Cheryl Charming presides over this classy spot on Bourbon (one of the few left), and her gin fizz can be ordered shaken for six or twelve minutes. Back in 1888, when bar owner Henry "Carl" Ramos invented this mix of citrus, gin, egg white, and orange flower water, shaker boys did the job. Charming's version benefits from an automatic shaker contraption that whips the fizz into an ethereal frenzy sure to leave telltale traces on your upper lip.

730 Bourbon St., 504-571-4685
bourbono.com

TIP

Another storied Ramos Gin Fizz can be had at the genteel Victorian Lounge in the Garden District's Columns Hotel, an authentic, old-time bar experience complete with cocktails retro and nuevo.

3811 St. Charles Ave., 504-899-9308
thecolumns.com

ORDER A SAZERAC
AT SAZERAC BAR

Cocktail wags largely agree that the Sazerac is one of the oldest examples of the American cocktail. Smoky, slightly sweet with just an insinuation of bitterness, the drink itself is downright simple. Good rye whisky, Peychaud's bitters, sugar, a chilled glass rinsed with absinthe, and a healthy dose of oil from a wide ribbon of lemon peel sets the stage for perfection. Worship at the altar of Sazerac at the impeccable Sazerac Bar in the gorgeous Roosevelt Hotel, where the nineteenth-century original recipe is favored. The place is simply elegant, with an impressive African walnut bar bordered by original Paul Ninas murals. It all adds up to a throwback to a gentler age, made even better with a Sazerac in hand.

130 Roosevelt Way, 504-648-1200
therooseveltneworleans.com

RESERVE A TABLE
AT SHAYA

The hottest table in New Orleans isn't at one of the storied Creole palaces dishing buttery trout amandine and oysters Rockefeller. Instead, the toughest reservation to snag is at Shaya, a modern Israeli eatery where hummus reigns supreme, and avocado toast keeps company with smoky whitefish and zippy bits of pink peppercorns. Chef Alon Shaya casts a flavorful gaze to his native Israel, creating umami combinations with the likes of pureed chickpeas, tahini, Aleppo pepper, and fragrant olive oil. The fried cauliflower, crispy and dusted with curry, and the ground lamb ragu peppered with pine nuts are two winning options. And for dessert, order the exotic malabi, an ethereal vanilla custard that tastes like a walk through a tropical garden.

4213 Magazine St., 504-891-4213
shayarestaurant.com

GET YOUR JUST DESSERTS
AT SUCRE

Tariq Hanna is an artist, and his medium is sugar. Find out for yourself at Sucre, his sweet retreat filled with gossamer macarons, Italian gelatos, and chocolates that stand up to the best in Belgium. The Dark Chocolate Bark, sheets of chocolate shot through with assorted nuts and dried fruits, is a must-taste, as is the Drinking Chocolate, which is served with handmade marshmallows and caramel cookies for dipping. The original mint green jewel box in the Garden District is beautifully appointed, an ideal place for a treat while shopping Magazine. Hanna's French Quarter location offers sweets on the first floor, but upstairs at Salon by Sucre well-crafted cocktails and artful savories await. Sweeten the experience by dining on the balcony overlooking the city.

Sucre
3025 Magazine St., 504-520-8311
shopsucre.com

Salon by Sucre
622 Conti St., 504-267-7098
restaurantsalon.com

SIP SPIRITS
AT TALES OF THE COCKTAIL

What brings twenty thousand superstar bartenders, liquor brand managers, artisanal distillers, and serious imbibers to steamy New Orleans the third week of July? Tales of the Cocktail, that's what, a week of seminars, tastings, networking events, and parties that make Tales THE place to set and catch craft cocktail trends, bar none. Founded in 2002, Tales of the Cocktail has grown into the world's premier festival celebrating all things shaken and stirred, a series of ticketed events from lectures to dinner pairings, cooking and shaking demos, and more, all aimed at industry insiders as well as foodies and cocktail enthusiasts. Sign up for a seminar (The Drunken Botanist perhaps?), attend a whiskey-themed dinner, and slurp a bracing spritz made with Amaro with a group of Italians. Sounds fun, right?

538 Louisa St., 504-948-0511
talesofthecocktail.com

GO ON
A FOODIE RAMBLE OR RIDE

Eating your way through New Orleans's 1,300+ restaurants takes a commitment. Concentrated grazing by culinary tour is the answer. Confederacy of Cruisers in the Marigny offers a fab Culinary Bike Tour, an easy pedal between downhome dishes in neighborhoods all over town. Destination Kitchen Food Tours showcases deliciousness uptown on Oak Street and St. Charles Avenue in the Garden District, along with strolls in the French Quarter, with or without a cooking experience. Julie Barreda Bruyn offers tours in English, French, or Spanish—three languages that New Orleans has spoken for centuries. New Orleans Culinary History Tours feasts on local specialties spiced with plenty of backstory. Whether regaling tales of the Quarter's iconic Creole restaurants or focusing on historic cocktailing, this guided experience delivers.

Confederacy of Cruisers
634 Elysian Fields Ave., 504-400-5468
confederacyofcruisers.com

Destination Kitchen Food Tours
855-DK-Foodie or 855-353-6634
foodtoursneworleans.com

New Orleans Culinary History Tours
504-875-6570
noculinarytours.com

FEEL SPECIAL
AT THE UPPERLINE

Gracious owner JoAnn Clevenger makes everyone feel at home at her cozy uptown restaurant, located in a restored nineteenth-century home brimming with local art. Chef Trent Osborne took over the kitchen in 2014 and is walking just the right balance between respecting the timeless dishes that regulars crave and bringing new inspired creations to the table. The drum piquant with hot & hot shrimp will never leave the menu, same for the slow-roasted half duckling with garlic port sauce, spotlighted by chef Aaron Sanchez on the show *Best Thing I Ever Ate*. But you might find something such as tempura baby eggplant smothered in ginger "barbecue" blue crab as a special, a sign that this uptown restaurant is always cooking something up.

1413 Upperline St., 504-891-9822
upperline.com

Photo Credit: LouisianaNorthshore.com

MUSIC AND ENTERTAINMENT

DANCE YOUR PANTS OFF
TO KERMIT RUFFINS

"We partying!" is Kermit Ruffins's mantra, a shout-out interjected frequently during his rousing performance, all sass and brass, with the local trumpet player and singer channeling the great Louis Armstrong and a litany of New Orleans standards during a typical bet-you-can't-sit-down show. The New Orleans native and Basin Street Records recording artist, who cofounded Rebirth Brass Band in 1983, had a standing late-night gig every Thursday at Vaughan's in the Bywater for twenty years. Ruffins plays earlier shows these days at various clubs, including Bullet's Sports Bar in Treme and Little Gem Saloon in the CBD and most Fridays at Blue Nile. Or you can catch him at his own club, Kermit's Treme Mother-in-Law Lounge, formerly home base to the infamous Ernie K-Doe. Wherever you hear him, Kermit always delivers a good time.

Little Gem Saloon
445 S. Rampart St., 504-267-4863
littlegemsaloon.com

Kermit's Treme
Mother-in-Law Lounge
1500 N. Claiborne Ave.,
504-814-1819

Bullet's Sports Bar
2441 A. P. Tureaud Ave.,
504-669-4464

Blue Nile
532 Frenchmen St.,
504-948-2583
bluenilelive.com

RELIVE THE '80S
AT ONE EYED JACKS

In a town full of cool music venues, One Eyed Jacks manages to make an impression. A local haunt since it was the Shim-Sham Club, this French Quarter darling is known for its early bordello décor (love the red velvet curtains and chandeliers), great dance floor, and wildly eclectic music offerings. An intimate venue for everything from heavy metal to burlesque, the club's Thursday night '80s dance party is a can't-sit-down bash. Attracting a group of straight and gay regulars often decked out in shoulder pads and vinyl, the music is a nonstop tribute to glam bands and big hair. You know you secretly want to dance to "Jessie's Girl." What are you waiting for? This place rocks.

615 Toulouse St., 504-569-8361
oneeyedjacks.net

PARTY DOWN
BOURBON STREET

Although locals often cast a baleful glance at Bourbon Street, the famous party street attracts millions from around the world to its nearly mile-long stretch of honky-tonks, souvenir shops, strip clubs, and restaurants. While mostly geared to tourists and convention goers in search of scintillation and libation, Bourbon can deliver a lighthearted romp perfect for an uninhibited good time. With open container laws encouraging walking and drinking, famously potent drinks, such as Hurricanes, Hand Grenades, and frozen daiquiris, make the leap to letting loose a short one. Whether it's Mardi Gras season or a regular midsummer week, balconies overflow with partygoers ready to toss beads to throngs below.

PAY HOMAGE TO
A BOURBON STREET ICON

On a street more honky-tonk than real deal, Chris Owens stands alone. Owens, a tall drink of Texas water in her eighth decade, is a Bourbon Street icon, a whirling dervish of sequins, song, and dance. Backed by her outstanding house band, the singer's endless legs keep the beat to everything from salsa to disco, and while her vocals may be a bit throaty, there's no mistaking a show biz pro once she takes the stage. Sporting a mane of cascading black curls, Owens shimmies and parades like it's Mardi Gras morning, delivering the kind of fabulous floor show that used to be the norm on Bourbon Street before strip clubs and T-shirt shops took over the landscape.

500 Bourbon St., 504-523-6400
chrisowensclub.net

TIP

While most Bourbon Street venues are geared to drink-guzzling tourists, real music fans know that Fritzel's Jazz Pub and Irvin Mayfield's Jazz Playhouse represent authentic New Orleans music.

Fritzel's Jazz Pub
733 Bourbon St., 504 586-4800
fritzelsjazz.net

Irvin Mayfield's Jazz Playhouse
300 Bourbon St., 504-553-2299
irvinmayfield.com

CATCH JON CLEARY
AT CHICKIE WAH WAH

When he's not touring the world, this Grammy-winning singer and blues piano player from the UK plays most Tuesdays in his Mid-City neighborhood at Chickie Wah Wah on Canal Street, a venue known for letting artists set and keep the cover charge at the door. Cleary works with a killer band, the Absolute Monster Gentlemen, but his star turn at Chickie Wah Wah is just his bad funky self on piano. His deeply soulful vocals, songwriting skills, and spot on musicianship have made Cleary a respected peer of such R&B legends as Dr. John and the late, great Allen Toussaint, who did much of the arranging on Cleary's Grammy-winning 2016 album *Gogo Juice* on FHQ Records. This club attracts a slightly older crowd of music lovers, a welcome change for the over-forty set.

2828 Canal St., 844-244-2543
chickiewahwah.com

CLUB HOP
ON ST. CLAUDE AVENUE

Locals of a certain mind-set in search of an alternative to Frenchmen Street have the artsy St. Claude Corridor firmly in their sights. Rooted in the city's post-Katrina influx of artists and new residents, this emerging avenue, known as Good Children until 1850, is just a stroll away from the Marigny, extending three miles from Esplanade Avenue past the Bywater to the Industrial Cana. In recent years, an exploding number of pubs, theaters, and restaurants have joined such institutional venues as Saturn Bar to create a Nuevo New Orleans dining and entertainment destination, now at least partially accessible by the new streetcar line. The Hi Ho, Kajun's Pub, Siberia, Sweet Lorraine's, and the Allways Lounge deliver a mixed bag of comedy, klezmer, bluegrass, boy-lesque, and karaoke within a few blocks' radius every night of the week.

The Hi Ho
2239 St. Claude Ave., 504-945-4446
hiholounge.net

Sweet Lorraine's Jazz Club
1931 St. Claude Ave.,
504-945-9654

Kajun's Pub
2256 St. Claude Ave., 504-947-3735
kajunpub.com

Siberia Lounge
2227 St. Claude Ave.,
504-265-8855
siberianola.com

The Allways Lounge
2240 St. Claude Ave., 504-218-5778
http://theallwayslounge.net

DROP BY THE DEW DROP JAZZ & SOCIAL HALL
ACROSS THE LAKE

Of the myriad reasons to cross Lake Pontchartrain to the Northshore, the Dew Drop Jazz & Social Hall tops the list. Founded by the Dew Drop Social and Benevolent Association and built in 1895—the same year scholars say jazz with born in New Orleans—the unpainted hall on Lamarque Street, nestled in a grove of ancient live oaks, is considered the world's oldest virtually unaltered rural jazz dance hall. A major hub for African American jazz musicians during the 1920s and '30s, its modest stage held the likes of Kid Ory, Bunk Johnson, and quite possibly Satchmo himself. The Dew Drop is now a nonprofit with shows fall through spring, generally acoustic performances by candlelight or under the stars, with music wafting from the open windows as it has since the last two centuries.

430 Lamarque St., Old Mandeville
dewdropjazzhall.com

FESTIVAL HOP
ALL YEAR LONG

New Orleans may well have invented the festival. This is a town that throws parties to honor the homely mirliton and local Creole tomato. We celebrate oysters, fried chicken, gumbo, and Louisiana seafood. Neighborhood fetes abound, with feet dancing from the Treme to uptown on Freret. Diversity is heralded at Greek Fest, Southern Decadence, and Soul Fest. Local art, live music, and good eats are the common denominator, and entrance is usually free. If there is a charge, it's for good at fund-raisers, such as Hogs for the Cause and Emeril's Boudin, Bourbon, and Beer. Dedicated music festivals of note include Satchmo Summer Fest, French Quarter Fest, Essence, and the Voodoo Music + Arts Experience. Art lovers gallery-hop on White Linen and Dirty Linen nights, the Tennessee Williams/New Orleans Literary Festival inspires word play, and the New Orleans Film Festival draws rave reviews.

KEEP THE FREE BEAT
ON THE STREET

Walking along the Mississippi to the soulful tune of a lone sax player is a quintessential New Orleans moment. In this vibrant city known around the world as a music mecca, a deep pool of talent not only energizes the club scene but also enervates sidewalks from Royal to Frenchmen Street. Playing to an all-ages crowd, unlike the 21-and-over bar and club audience, street buskers can be found during the day in the 300-800 blocks of Royal Street, with such regulars as Doreen's Jazz, usually camped out in front of Rouse's Supermarket. Come evening, famous Frenchmen Street is alive with raucous corner brass bands, but really any old time along the river and around Jackson Square in the French Quarter, you'll hear musicians making a joyful noise.

TUNE IN
TO THE MUSIC SCENE
ON FRENCHMEN STREET

Frenchmen Street in the Marigny is hands down one of the best concentrations of live music venues in town. Every night within a three-block stretch you can second line with a brass band, catch a reggae groove at Cafe Negril, and swing dance at the Spotted Cat. Next door there's an evening art garden spotlighting local talent. A few doors up, hear excellent funk at Blue Nile with Big Sam's Funky Nation, and support such local talent as Washboard Chaz at the Apple Barrel. Ellis Marsalis is a Friday regular at Snug Harbor, a stellar jazz venue. Cover charges vary, but it's free to wander the street and people watch, music pouring out of clubs as you stroll.

Apple Barrel Bar
609 Frenchmen St., 504- 949-9399

Cafe Negril
606 Frenchmen St., 504- 944-4744
cafenegrilonfrenchmen.com

Spotted Cat
623 Frenchmen St., 504-943-3887
spottedcatmusicclub.com

Snug Harbor
626 Frenchmen St., 504-949-0696
snugjazz.com

Blue Nile
532 Frenchman St., 504-948-2583
bluenilelive.com

JOIN THE CROWD
AT JAZZ FEST

The annual New Orleans Jazz & Heritage music festival, first held in Congo Square in 1970, now draws close to a half million attendees over the course of seven days in late April and early May. What's so special about Jazz Fest? Depending on whom you talk to, it's a tie between the music and the food, followed by (in no particular order) the people watching, the after-fest shows around town, and did we mention the food? Held on the oval of the Fair Grounds Race Course, a horse track that can be quite pungent when muddied, Jazz Fest is an annual tradition for a legion of locals and fans from all over the world, drawn together by a love of jazz and blues, Zydeco and gospel, and boiled crawfish washed down with plenty of beer.

nojazzfest.com

SETTLE IN
AT SNUG FOR REAL-DEAL JAZZ

Frenchmen Street is a nonstop party powered by raucous crowds intent on drinking and dancing to live music. Head away from the noise, and take shelter at Snug Harbor, a place where grown-ups and music fans pay attention to the art of jazz. Not that all of the acts are old school, although patriarch Ellis Marsalis presides onstage most Fridays, always a classy treat. Charmaine Neville is up Mondays, scatting her rootsy take on standards and New Orleans favorites. Or you might catch the jazzy Stanton Moore Trio one night, spotlighting the talented drummer out of his usual Galactic milieu. There's a solid menu of eats, a good bar, and best of all the space to relax and listen as some of the city's best musicians work their magic.

626 Frenchmen St., 504-949-0696
snugjazz.com

CLAP YOUR HANDS
AT THE HALL

If a venue can be a museum, if a living art form can transform, if music can speak all languages, it's at Preservation Hall in the French Quarter. The internationally known landmark may not look like much at first glance, and those bench seats are anything but comfortable, but Preservation Hall is the ultimate for music fans interested in traditional New Orleans–style jazz. Folks start lining up early to get a general admission seat, or you can pay a little more online to guarantee a spot. The Hall is also one of the few family-friendly jazz joints in town, with three shows seven nights a week. There's no AC, bar, or drinking (or talking) during the show. This place is all about preserving New Orleans jazz and has been since 1961.

726 St. Peter St., 504-522-2841
preservationhall.com

STAY UP LATE WITH REBIRTH
AT THE MAPLE LEAF

Rebirth Brass was founded in 1983 on the notion that New Orleans brass doesn't come in just one flavor. The band, known for its legendary Tuesday late-night gig at the Maple Leaf uptown on Oak Street, both upholds the tradition of brass and plays it forward, bringing funk and hip-hop into the mix. The Grammy-winning result is epic and so New Orleans, a booty-shaking party in motion that transforms Tuesday night into a happening. The Maple Leaf, an institution since 1974, is one of the longest running New Orleans music clubs, with live performances seven nights a week crossing all musical styles, from blues, funk, and R&B to rock, Zydeco, and jazz. The place is cool, drawing lively crowds that usually spill out onto the street.

8316 Oak St., 504-866-9359
mapleleafbar.com

TIP
Line up early for massive portions of Creole soul food at the always-quirky Jacques-Imo's, a few doors up from the Leaf.

8324 Oak St., 504-861-0886
jacques-imos.com

STRIKE OUT
FOR ROCK 'N' BOWL

Live music and bowling? The combination is a match made in heaven at Rock 'n' Bowl, the best bowling alley/music venue on the planet. Kick up your heels to live rock, R&B, swing, jazz, and blues with the clamor of rolling balls and falling pins for added syncopation. Thursday is Zydeco night, a hugely popular dance event with a legion of local fans. An institution since John Blancher opened in 1993, Rock 'n' Bowl changed locations in 2005, taking over a former grocery store across from Ye Olde College Inn, a homey Creole restaurant also run by the talented Blancher family. Locals wax nostalgic about the original, but the spirit of Rock 'n' Bowl still has plenty of funk to spare.

Rock 'n' Bowl
3016 S. Carrollton Ave., 504-861-1700
rocknbowl.com

Ye Olde College Inn
3000 S. Carrollton Ave., 504-866-3683
collegeinn1933.com

SPACE OUT
AT THE SATURN BAR

This quintessential dive predates the current St. Claude Avenue trending by decades. Mick Jagger partied at the Saturn Bar before he was collecting Social Security for heaven's sake. The place always looks closed, but don't let the haunted house exterior scare you off. Inside you'll find feisty bartenders, grand graffiti, and on one Saturday a month, an epic Mod Dance Party with DJ Matty spinning soul, garage, and British invasion tunes all night long. Co-owner Bailee Broyard honors the memory of her late uncle O'Neill, who opened the Saturn in the '60s, with an eclectic roster of local and touring acts along with extremely cold beer. The Saturn used to stand alone, but in a flurry of recent development, restaurants, including Sugar Park and Red's Chinese, have opened across the street.

Saturn Bar
3067 St. Claude Ave., 504-949-7532
saturnbar.com

Red's Chinese
3048 St. Claude Ave., 504-304-6030
redschinese.com

Sugar Park
3054 St. Claude Ave., 504-942-2047
sugarparknola.com

RUB PROFESSOR LONGHAIR'S HEAD
FOR LUCK AT TIP'S

On your way into Tipitina's, the legendary uptown juke joint famous for rocking the rafters, give the bust of New Orleans pianist Professor Longhair a rub for luck. You're already lucky and smart to party at this funky dance hall, a beloved locals' fave instrumental in launching the careers of many artists, including the Neville Brothers, Harry Connick Jr., Dr. John, and the subdudes. Rocking strong since 1977, Tip's presents both local and touring acts crossing all genres, with free Sunday afternoon shows spotlighting emerging artists. Friday shows are free during the summer months, an initiative of the Tipitina's Foundation, staying true to its mission to preserve Louisiana's and New Orleans's irreplaceable music community.

501 Napoleon Ave., 504-566-7095
tipitinas.com

SHAKE IT TO THE TREME BRASS BAND
AT THE CANDLELIGHT

The Treme Brass Band epitomizes the New Orleans sound, a rousing horns-forward marching band led by snare drummer Benny Jones Sr. with a roster of performers that has included Kermit Ruffins and the late Uncle Lionel Batiste. Featured on the original soundtrack of the HBO series *Treme*, Treme Brass plays most Wednesdays at the Candlelight Lounge, a no-frills neighborhood institution on Robertson that recently got a bit of a redo. The group performs from 9 p.m.(ish) to midnight, and red beans and rice is free to all comers. (Don't forget to tip.) You can also catch Corey Henry and his crew The Treme Funktet Band most Sunday evenings. The Candlelight is also a favorite stop during second line parades, but really any time is Candlelight time.

925 N Robertson St., 504-525-4748

SPORTS AND RECREATION

CHEER THE SAINTS OR CATCH A SHOW
IN THE DOME

The Mercedes-Benz Superdome is the highlight of the New Orleans skyline, with its instantly recognizable design looking like an alien spaceship parked in the middle of downtown. The site of the annual Sugar Bowl, the Dome is most importantly home to the city's beloved football team, the New Orleans Saints, forever credited with making a city still recovering after Katrina feel like a winner with a 2009 Super Bowl victory. With seating for more than 70,000 and no bad seat in the house, the Dome hosts the city's largest music concerts, expositions, and festivals. Performers from Beyonce to the late, great Prince have commanded the stage. Saints fans put on their own show during home games, tailgating around the Dome with the enthusiasm of true believers.

1500 Sugar Bowl Dr., 504-587-3663
mbsuperdome.com

KAYAK BAYOU
ST. JOHN

A snowy egret watches cagily from the banks of Bayou St. John, strutting with his oversized yellow feet like a clown on parade. Maybe he's not used to seeing humans kayaking in his urban waterway, a sight that's becoming increasingly common, thanks to Kayak-iti-Yat, a business owned by local partners Sara Howard and Sonny Averett. Founded in 2011, Kayak-iti-Yat (a paddling riff on the local query, "Where y'at?") offers a new perspective on the city's charming Mid-City neighborhood bounded by the historic canal, once a vibrant transportation waterway connecting to Lake Pontchartrain. The tour includes bits of history and lore shouted into the breeze, historic homes are identified, and a growing confluence of birds remarked upon, from great blue herons to beady-eyed pelicans.

3494 Esplanade Ave., 985-778-5034
kayakitiyat.com

TAKE THE FERRY
TO GET TO THE POINT

Although locals still grouse after so many years of free rides, the ferry across the Mississippi River to historic Algiers Point is a heckuva deal. For $2 each way, you can get the absolute best view of the city skyline as you follow the river's dramatic crescent bend. Weaving through the traffic that makes the Mississippi the hardest working river in the nation, the double-decker ferry leaves you at Algiers Point, the second-oldest neighborhood in New Orleans, with a village vibe that's sure to charm. Take a self-guided tour of the Jazz Walk of Fame along the levee, pop into local shops, and have a drink at the Old Point, a friendly watering hole with live music on the weekends.

Canal Street at the Mississippi
504-309-9789
nolaferries.com

Old Point Bar
545 Patterson Dr., 504-364-0950
oldpointbarnola.com

Algiers Point Association
algierspoint.org

BIKE ON THE LEVEE
TO RIVERTOWN

An abandoned country club, swimming pools above ground and below, horse stables, a chicken coop, kids playing, dogs being walked, huge freighters navigating the river, planes taking off and landing. Those are just a few of the sights you'll see cycling along the Mississippi River Trail on the levee from the zoo at Audubon Park all the way to Rivertown in Kenner. Also known in cycling circles as the levee bike path, the 22-mile flat, paved trail is usually free of crossing traffic on the weekends, making this a popular training route. But don't go too fast, because you'll miss the views along the way, cruising along with the mighty river on one side and scenes of industry and family life on the other.

TIP

Four more rides to try: 15 miles along Lakeshore Drive; the 31-mile rails-to-trails Tammany Trace on the Northshore; 2.6 miles between Treme and Lakeview on the Lafitte Greenway, and an easy 1.4-mile cruise in Crescent Park, with river views between the French Quarter and Bywater.

CROSS THE CAUSEWAY BRIDGE
FOR A CHANGE

New Orleanians have been recreating on the north shore of Lake Pontchartrain since the antebellum years, when the locals flocked to "l'autre cote du lac" (the other side of the lake) for fresh air and wholesome pursuits. The game-changing 24-mile Lake Pontchartrain Causeway opened in 1956, cutting the commute from New Orleans to forty-five minutes and transforming the sleepy towns of St. Tammany Parish—Abita Springs, Covington, Folsom, Lacombe, Madisonville, Mandeville, and Slidell—into bedroom communities for the Big Easy. Cross the causeway, with pelicans and dolphins for company, and then stay a spell on the Northshore, where you can feed giraffes at Global Wildlife Center, tour the local Abita Brewing Company, visit a working alligator ranch, and shop and dine amidst small-town charm.

Insta-Gator Ranch & Hatchery
4645 Allen Rd., Covington,
985-892-3669
insta-gatorranch.com

Global Wildlife Center
26389 Louisiana 40, Folsom,
985-798-3585
globalwildlife.com

Abita Brewing Company
66 Barbee Rd., Covington,
800-737-2311
abita.com/visit/tours

Louisiana's Northshore
louisiananorthshore.com

SNEAK UP ON A TURTLE
IN CITY PARK

For locals who don't have lots of personal green space, City Park is an extended backyard, a place to picnic and barbecue, bike, and fritter away a lazy afternoon. The 1,300-acre Eden known for its stands of live oak trees and outdoor recreation includes a manmade lake with kayaks and stand-up paddleboards for rent. Walk around the lake and keep your eyes peeled for yellow-footed egrets and snoozing turtles sunning on the trunks of palms reaching over the water. There's a real Venetian gondola for hire, piloted by a Cajun guy who learned the trade in Venice. The park includes the New Orleans Museum of Art, with its free outdoor sculpture garden, City Bark for doggies, as well as a play area for kids and an antique carousel. It's a wondrous place.

504-482-4888
neworleanscitypark.com

CLIMB
MONKEY HILL

When you grow up below sea level, running up a hill is a startling experience, which is why Monkey Hill in Audubon Zoo has been a favorite play spot for more than eight decades. Created in 1934 by the dirt claimed from the digging of a 1,200-foot-long lagoon to form the zoo's water features, Monkey Hill originally rose an impressive 30-ish feet in the air, a veritable Everest to peanut-sized climbers. Just like people tend to do, the hill has lost a few inches as it has aged, but the zoo has added improvements, including a five-level tree house, a slide, bronze lion sculptures for climbing, and wading pools to splash in. There's still plenty of room to roll down Monkey Hill, a highlight of a zoo visit for generations.

6500 Magazine St., 504-861-2537
audubonnatureinstitute.org/zoo

CHILL ON THE RIVER
AT THE FLY

Tucked behind Audubon Zoo across the Mississippi River levee, the Fly is a strip of frontage high enough to actually deliver river views, an anomaly in a city built below sea level. Named for a mostly forgotten butterfly-shaped river viewing shelter built in the 1960s and demolished in the 1980s, the Fly is a beehive of activity when the weather is fine. This swath of riverfront green space is the go-to spot for softball and kickball games, family barbecues, Frisbee throws, and crawfish boils. It's also fun to just sit and watch the river traffic, an endless flow of commercial barges and ships from exotic ports of call. Dusk is an enchanting time of day as the sun sets over the river, a spectacular sight, especially over a shared bottle of wine.

River Drive, behind the Audubon Zoo

WATCH SAILBOATS, PELICANS, AND FISHING
AT THE LAKE

There is no better place to watch the sun go down than along Lakeshore Drive facing Lake Pontchartrain. With newly redone hardscaping, benches, and picnic pavilions, all since Katrina, the scenic drive along the south shore of the lakefront is more accessible than ever before. A gathering place for couples and families, it's not uncommon to see picnickers sharing a bottle of wine and cheese, friends drinking daiquiris and eating take-out, and fisherman reeling in catfish for dinner. There are benches for sitting awhile and paths for meandering, views of sailboats and swooping pelicans, creating a serene tableau. A cluster of seafood restaurants sits on the Canal Street end of the lake, places such as the Blue Crab and Landry's, where raw oysters and shrimp etoufee are served with a lake view.

The Blue Crab
7900 Lakeshore Dr., 504-284-2898
thebluecrabnola.com

Landry's
8000 Lakeshore Dr., 504-283-1010
landryseafood.com

JOG, WALK, OR CRAWL
IN THE RED DRESS RUN

Staged by the New Orleans Hash House Harriers, a self-proclaimed "drinking club with a running problem," the annual Red Dress Run has raised more than $1 million to date for a hundred local charities. Taking place on the steamy second Saturday in August, the two-mile run through the French Quarter from Armstrong Park isn't really about running. At the 11 a.m. start in 2016, only a handful of crimson-clad joggers and walkers even gathered at the starting line. Most of the burly dudes hilariously outfitted in flowing red garb were already in their cups, drinking free-flowing beer and generally having a great time. The party starts early and includes food and live music and always spills out into the French Quarter, where red-frocked "runners" can be found partying until the wee hours.

The New Orleans Hash House Harriers
noh3.com

Red Dress Run
nolareddress.com

SLEEP
ON THE LAKE

Imagine sleeping on a stilted cottage built over the water, the sound of lapping waves lulling you to sleep. You don't have to go to the South Pacific for this experience—just cross the 24-mile Causeway Bridge to the Northshore, and head for Fontainebleau State Park. Centrally located not far from the sweet downtowns of Covington and Mandeville, this 2,800-acre park includes twelve cabins built over Pontchartrain in the middle of glorious nature. Treated to a $1.5 million redo after Hurricane Isaac, the cottages are furnished for comfort with flat-screen TVs, screened porches, and fully equipped kitchens, ideal for a family getaway. Make your reservation early, and while you're at it, set up dinner at John Besh's fantastic La Provence restaurant nearby, a rustic auberge specializing in farm-to-table French-Creole cuisine.

La Provence
25020 US-190, Lacombe, 985-626-7662
laprovencerestaurant.com

Fontainebleau State Park
2883 Louisiana 1089, Mandeville,
985-624-4443
fontainebleaustatepark.com

SPY GATORS
ON THEIR HOME TURF

Scores of tours are available that explore the bayous an hour or so outside of New Orleans, but Honey Island Swamp Tours and Pearl River Eco-Tours are two of the best. Located in Slidell, Honey Island Swamp Tours was founded by wetland ecologist Dr. Paul Wagner in 1982. Wagner and his staff lead fascinating tours of the protected swamp, home to spectacular wildlife, including alligators, waterfowl, nutria, and turtles. Pearl River Eco-Tours, owned and operated by Captain Neil Benson, also explores the Honey Island Swamp, using smaller boats than the big tour operators for a more intimate bayou experience. Benson grew up camping and fishing here and is passionate about preserving its lush beauty. Both trips will leave you with a deeper understanding of local wildlife and swamp ecology.

Honey Island Swamp Tours
504-242-5877 or 985-641-1769
honeyislandswamp.com

Pearl River Eco-Tours
55050 Hwy. 90, Slidell, 985-649-4200
pearlriverecotours.com

HAVE TURKEY DINNER
AT THE TRACK

To the thousands of music fans that storm the Fair Grounds Race Course during Jazz Fest, the track is the setting for a blowout music and food festival. For the many longtime horseracing fans who frequent the Fair Grounds, which dates back to 1852, the one-mile dirt oval is the backdrop for thrilling thoroughbred competition and wagering. Thanksgiving is opening day for the racing season, creating a holiday tradition for generations of New Orleanians that is anything but Rockwellian. A crowd of 7,000+ typically spends Thanksgiving at the track, passing the stuffing in the upscale Clubhouse Dining Room, a space that sells out months in advance. There's also a Thanksgiving buffet served in the Grandstand, where jockeying for a drumstick isn't the only game in town.

1751 Gentilly Blvd., 504-944-5518
fairgroundsracecourse.com

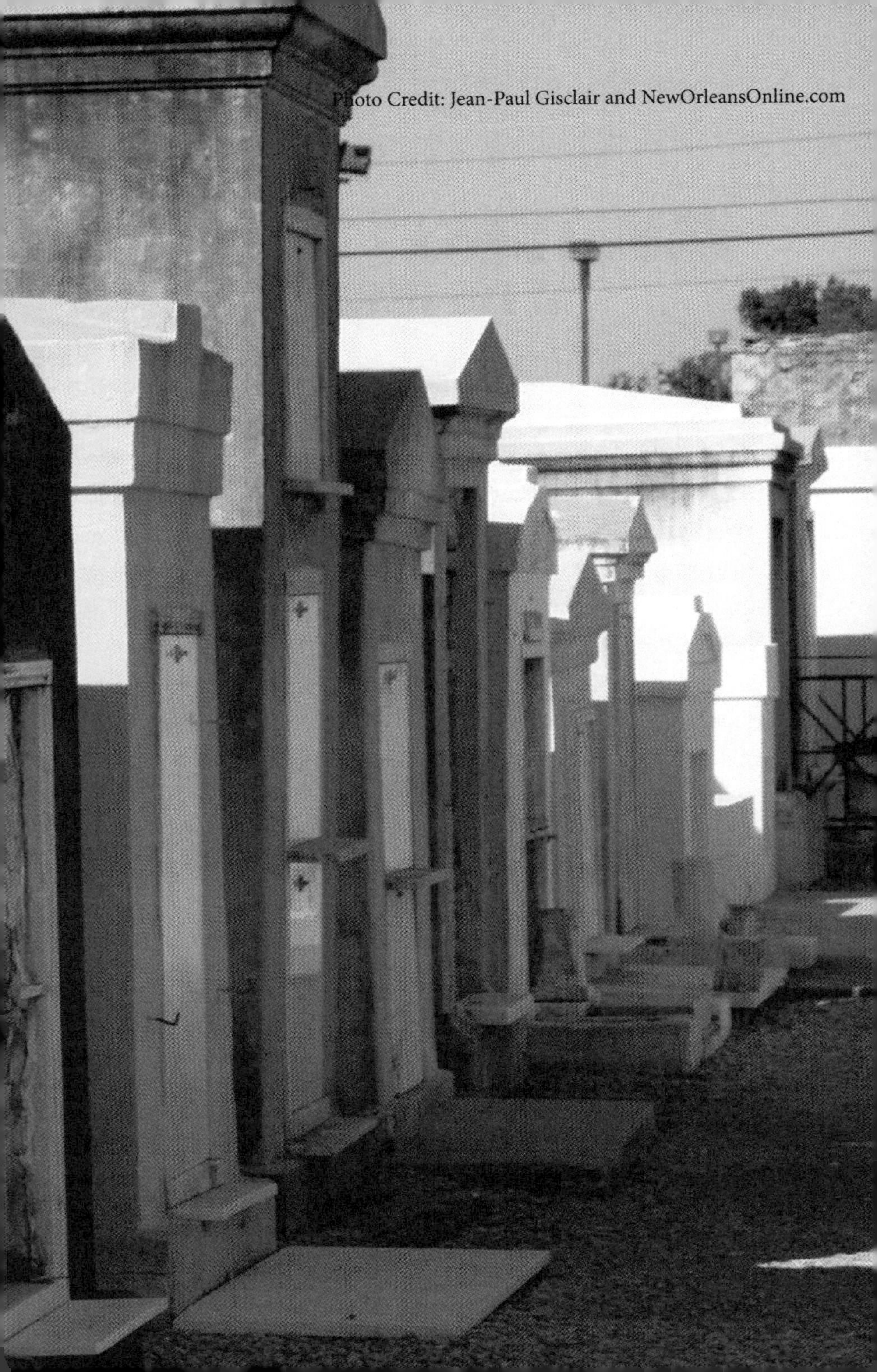

Photo Credit: Jean-Paul Gisclair and NewOrleansOnline.com

CULTURE AND HISTORY

TOUR THE LEAFY
GARDEN DISTRICT

Excluded from early nineteenth-century French and Creole society, Yankee newcomers got busy creating their own city. That neighborhood of wrought iron fences, exquisite gardens, and lush antebellum homes define what is now the Garden District, an area bordered by St. Charles Avenue and Magazine Street, and Jackson Avenue to Louisiana Avenue. Originally home to the city's plantation owners and shipping magnates, the Garden District remains rich in Greek Revival architecture, a point underscored by streets named for the nine Muses of Greek mythology. Take the St. Charles Avenue streetcar to Washington Avenue, where the elegantly teal Commander's Palace awaits, along with the famous Lafayette Cemetery #1 across the street. Bus, carriage, or walking tours of the neighborhood are offered daily. Or simply stroll the oak-lined avenues on your own.

TIP

A Hop-On, Hop-Off Bus Tour delivers great overviews of the city on an open-air double decker bus and your ticket includes free walking tours of the Garden District, Lafayette Cemetery #1, and the French Quarter.

citysightseeingneworleans.com

TIP

Find the Brevard-Wisdom-Rice House at 1239 First Street, a columned beauty that sheltered horror yarn spinner Anne Rice from 1989 to 2004. The author, who featured New Orleans as a backdrop in her best-selling *Vampire Chronicles,* used the house as a setting for her 1990 novel *The Witching Hour.*

PUSH ALL BOUNDARIES
AT KREWE DU VIEUX

After Joan of Arc rides through the Quarter on Twelfth Night, the big parade season kicks off with the always irreverent Krewe du Vieux. Taking place a few weeks before Mardi Gras Day, this satirical march through the Marigny is known for homemade, decorated hand-pulled or mule-drawn floats dripping with double entendre and in-your-face sassiness. Even the krewes' choice of royalty leans toward the funk, with the likes of Dr. John, Ernie K-Doe, and Big Freedia Queen of Bounce among the honorees. KDV is actually made up of thirty-odd (and odd is an understatement) subkrewes, with such names as Mishigas, Krewe of Spanks, and Drips & Discharges, each with their own interpretation of the year's theme, which in 2016 was "Krewe du Vieuxxx Rated XXX." Too much fun to miss.

kreweduvieux.org

SCARE YOURSELF SILLY
ON A HAUNTED GHOST TOUR

Arguably one of the most haunted cities in the world, New Orleans's ghosts are legend. Whether or not you're a believer in the afterworld, taking an after dark ghost tour is good eerie fun. Haunted History Tours and Free Tours by Foot are two excellent options for exploring the city's ghostly past, offering both over-the-top theatrics and historic commentary. For sure you'll hear blood-curdling tales of the atrocities that took place at the Lalaurie Mansion at 1140 Royal Street, famously bought but never lived in by oddball actor Nicolas Cage. You might tour one of the iconic cemeteries and even belly up at Lafitte's Blacksmith Shop Bar on the quiet side of Bourbon, where tales of the dead pirate are served with the beer.

Haunted History Tours
723 St. Peter St., 504-861-2727
hauntedhistorytours.com

Free Tours by Foot
504-222-2967
freetoursbyfoot.com

VISIT A WASHATERIA
MUSIC SHRINE

The average passerby wouldn't think twice about the ho-hum washateria at 838-840 North Rampart Street on the edge of the French Quarter, but a plaque outside The Clothes Spin and a display of historic photos inside reveal that between 1945 and 1957 this was the site of J&M Music Shop run by Cosimo Matassa, the penultimate shaper of the New Orleans R&B sound and some say the godfather of rock 'n' roll. A music producer and studio owner until he died in 2014, Matassa recorded some 250 singles and 21 gold records here, including "Tutti Frutti" by Little Richard, "Sea Cruise" by Frankie Ford, Aaron Neville's "Tell It Like It Is," and so many more.

840 N. Rampart St.,
504-522-1336

DIVE INTO HISTORY
AT CHALMETTE BATTLEFIELD

If you're like most people, what you know about the Battle of New Orleans came from a history book, but just seven miles downriver is where it all happened, the Chalmette Battlefield, and it's worth a visit. Start at the visitor center, where an excellent video recounts the battle; afterward, drive or walk the 1.5-mile road leading past re-created defenses extending from the Rodriguez Canal at the Mississippi River to what was then the tree line of the cypress swamp at the northern end of the battlefield.

The United States Civil War Chalmette National Cemetery is next to the battlefield, honoring Civil War soldiers who died on both sides. It holds only two American veterans from the Battle of New Orleans, but some 14,000 Union soldiers are buried here, including members of the legendary African American Buffalo Soldiers cavalry brigade.

8606 West St. Bernard Highway, Chalmette, 504-281-0510
nps.gov/jela/chalmette-battlefield.htm

GET DOWN AND DECADENT
AT SOUTHERN DECADENCE

Everybody in America celebrates the worker on Labor Day, the unofficial end of summer. In New Orleans, where sweltering temperatures continue for weeks, that same weekend is devoted to celebrating red-hot Southern Decadence. Also known as Gay Mardi Gras, Decadence is the ultimate in flamboyant fetes, an LGBTQ party that draws more than 100,000 revelers every year from around the world. Parties, DJs, parades, dances, and drag races all happen on the "quiet" end of Bourbon Street, with the Golden Lantern, a fab dive bar on the corner of Royal and Barracks, the unofficial headquarters. Catch the parade on Sunday, a wildly Technicolor affair with plenty of drag attire and boy-lesque. Grab a wig, wear something sequined and sassy, and order a cocktail. You'll fit right in.

southerndecadence.net

WANDER THE HISTORIC
FRENCH QUARTER

The French Quarter is the beating heart of New Orleans. From its Old World spirit to its cobblestone streets and faded elegance, the Quarter stands alone. What makes this neighborhood so unfailingly authentic is that it is just that—a neighborhood where people live, work, go to school, and take care of life's necessaries. They are just lucky enough to do it in the Vieux Carré, 120 jazz-soaked blocks rich with Spanish, French, Creole, and American architecture. The absolute best way, actually the only way, to explore the Quarter is on foot, a wander that delivers the pleasure of lush courtyards glimpsed through wrought iron gates and jasmine-scented air so sweet that it intoxicates. No matter how many times you walk it, there's always something magical to discover.

TIP

Show up at 9 a.m. Tuesday through Saturday at the French Quarter Visitor Center, 419 Decatur Street, and snag one of twenty-five free tickets to an hour-long neighborhood history walk along the Mississippi. First come, first served, and you can't beat the price.

GIDDY UP, BESSIE,
ON A MULE-DRAWN CARRIAGE RIDE

Jackson Square is the epicenter of street busking and sidewalk art in the French Quarter, a leafy park that's always buzzing with activity. Facing the Mississippi and directly across from St. Louis Cathedral, the Square is named for Andrew Jackson, whose statue depicts him sitting astride a rearing steed. Wander the square and rub elbows with artists *en plein air,* musicians, street performers, and tarot card readers. Mule-drawn carriages line up on the Decatur side of the square, ready to chauffeur you on a tour around town. Although the driver's commentary may not always stand up as truth in a court of law, the stories are colorful, and the clip-clop of mule hooves never fails to soothe.

neworleanscarriages.com

CELEBRATE MARDI GRAS
AT PARADES SMALL AND QUIRKY

Mardi Gras isn't only about the super krewes. For sheer underdog charm, there's the wonderful 'tit Rəx parade of shoebox-sized mini floats pulled from St. Roch Avenue into the Marigny. The Intergalactic Krewe of Chewbacchus is a sci-fi themed parade that steps off in the upper 9th and travels through the Marigny. Even if you're not a fan of the genre, you'll love the self-propelled float contraptions built onto bicycles, homemade trailers, and shopping carts. Canines star in the tail-wagging Barkus parade in the French Quarter, while on Mardi Gras Day, the brilliantly costumed march of Societé de Saint Anne draws throngs of costumed revelers, an array of nutty creatives who collect marchers from Bywater into the French Quarter, stopping at bars for celebrating along the way.

CELEBRATE
MARDI GRAS SUPERSIZED

New Orleanians understand that Mardi Gras, a season that begins Twelfth Night, January 6, and culminates on Fat Tuesday, the day before Ash Wednesday, is a marathon, not a sprint. Besides all the balls, parties, and king cake to eat, there are more than eighty parades in and around New Orleans, and it's impossible to catch them all. For carnival lovers, however, the three original super krewes—Orpheus, Endymion, and Bacchus—are at the top of the viewing list—spectacular parades known for intricate floats, high-tech wizardry, awesome throws, and grand costumes and themes. The all-female Nyx also claims super krewe status, rolling with more than thirty-five elaborate floats. The biggest parades feature celebrity kings and queens, with the likes of Kid Rock and Britney Spears holding court for a day.

TIP
Channel Carnival season year-round with a tour of Mardi Gras World, Blaine Kern's year-round float-building workshop.

http://www.mardigrasworld.com/

TRACE
THE HISTORY OF JAZZ
AT THE MINT

No matter how many millions were printed at the New Orleans Mint, the current collection of jazz memorabilia housed in this imposing red building on the downriver side of the French Quarter outdoes the cash as priceless treasure. Once a working branch of the U.S. Mint and now under the Louisiana State Museum umbrella, the museum contains irreplaceable musical instruments and related artifacts, including Louis Armstrong's first cornet, Sidney Bechet's soprano saxophone, Edward "Kid" Ory's trombone, George Lewis's clarinet, Warren "Baby" Dodds's drum kit, costumes, photographs, original manuscripts, historic recordings, and rare film footage. The city's jazz riches are staggering, which is reason enough for the launch of the official New Orleans Jazz Museum in the fall of 2017, a home for some 19,000 jazz-related artifacts to shine.

400 Esplanade Ave., 504-568-6993
louisianastatemuseum.org/museums/new-orleans-jazz-museum-the-old-us-mint

ROLL ON
DOWN THE RIVER

For a city that owes its life to the river, Mississippi experiences can be few and far between. That's why a ride on the Steamboat *Natchez* isn't just for tourists. A throwback to the days when steamboats cruised up and down the mighty Mississippi for commerce and pleasure, the *Natchez* reveals just how busy this working river remains. Traveling up and down the famed crescent bend, the *Natchez* serves straightforward Creole fare on lunch and dinner cruises, always with live jazz on board. But the food isn't the point here; instead, the kick is traveling the old-school way on the mighty Mississippi, sipping an excellent bloody Mary and dancing to the music of the Dukes of Dixieland, a brass forward jazz band that never disappoints.

Toulouse Street and the River, 504-586-8777
steamboatnatchez.com

TRAVEL BACK IN TIME
WITH THE HISTORIC NEW ORLEANS COLLECTION

Aimed squarely at lovers of New Orleans and history buffs, the Historic New Orleans Collection connects the dots in more than three centuries of city lore. A museum, research center, and publisher, the Collection was founded in 1966 to preserve the history and culture of New Orleans and the Gulf South. Located in a historic complex of French Quarter buildings, the Collection also includes an impressive staffed research center with an emphasis on rare books, maps, and plans relating to the Battle of New Orleans, one of the greatest military upsets of all time. You can also tour the historic Williams home, with its gorgeous antiques and Chinese porcelains. Don't bypass the shop. It's one of the best places to buy New Orleans–themed gifts.

533 Royal St., 504-523-4662
hnoc.org

HO-HO-HO
NEW ORLEANS STYLE

The 1955 Louis Armstrong carol "Christmas Time in New Orleans" is a brassy tribute to just how festive the holidays are in the Crescent City. Where else can you feast on Creole-inspired Reveillon dinners, warm to towering bonfires along the bayou, and sing carols on Jackson Square? Add in free concerts in St. Louis Cathedral, the family-geared hoopla of ChristmasFest complete with gingerbread houses and an ice rink at the Ernest N. Morial Convention Center, and the shimmering Christmas in the Oaks lights extravaganza in City Park, and New Orleans delivers holiday pageantry and then some. Because this is New Orleans, there has to be costumes, so a crowd of 4,000+ celebrants don Santa suits for the Annual Running of the Santas in the CBD. Now that's festive.

ChristmasFest
900 Convention Center Blvd., 855-477-8756
nolachristmasfest.com

New Orleans City Park
1 Victory Ave., 504-483-9415
neworleanscitypark.com/celebration-in-the-oaks

runningofthesantas.com

HEAR VOICES RAISED
AT THE ORPHEUM THEATER

New Orleans has seen a resurgence of theaters restored after the flood, but no space is more glorious than the Orpheum. Long considered the Carnegie Hall of the South, the Orpheum is home to the Louisiana Philharmonic as well as a mixed bag of concerts local and touring. Some $13 million went into restoring the 1918 Beaux Arts beauty, bringing the glimmer back to the gilded carved ceiling and the spring to the hardwood floor critical to the hall's stellar acoustics. There's not a bad seat in the 1,540-seat house, with pillar-free vertical design revealing a clear stage view at every tier. Climb to the vertiginous top level if heights thrill you to the core. Enjoy a drink at the bar along with oh-so-perfect aerial views of the action below.

129 Roosevelt Way, 504-274-4871
orpheumnola.com

CHANNEL SCARLETT AND RHETT
ON A PLANTATION TOUR

Harking back to the days when cotton was king and there were more millionaires in New Orleans than any other American city, the antebellum plantations along River Road offer windows into a bygone past. Each plantation tour offers stories told from varying perspectives, from Southern sugar barons to Creoles at Laura: A Creole Plantation, and at Whitney Plantation slaves are given a voice. For sheer beauty, visit Houmas House Plantation and Gardens, just forty-five minutes from New Orleans. A columned 1840 Greek Revival mansion straight out of *Gone With the Wind,* Houmas House is a stunner, with an alee of live oaks and gorgeous gardens. Stay overnight in a cottage and dine at Latil's Landing, an atmospheric 1770s French setting for chef Joseph Dicapo's imaginative cuisine.

Houmas House
40136 Highway 942, Darrow, LA,
225-473-9380
houmashouse.com

Laura: A Creole Plantation
2247 Highway 18, Vacherie, LA,
225-265-7690
lauraplantation.com

Whitney Plantation
5099 Highway 18, Wallace, LA,
225-265-3300
whitneyplantation.com

STRUT YOUR STUFF
IN A SECOND LINE

New Orleans's neighborhoods buzz with street life, from the stoop talk that connects friends and family to the second line parades that bring joyful roving block parties to all corners of the city. Second lines, rooted in nineteenth-century African American culture, are cousins to the city's famous jazz funerals, but you don't need a dearly departed to have one. Led by a brass band and a brightly festooned "first line" of paraders—the people who got the permit and the band—the second line is the folks who join the party, following the parade wherever it goes. You can catch second lines at such festivals as the Jazz Fest and Satchmo Fest, or check in with WWOZ 90.7 FM DJ Action Jackson, who lists second lines on his weekly show and the station's website.

wwoz.org/programs/inthestreet

WORSHIP
AT AN ALTAR OF FOOD

It's no surprise that in New Orleans, a historically Catholic city with strong Sicilian roots, St. Joseph's Day is a big deal. Add in that locals love food above all else, and worshipping at an elaborate altar made of pastry, fruit, and bread makes perfect sense. Celebrated March 19, the ritual commemorates the relief St. Joseph provided during a famine in Sicily, gratitude that was imported by the Sicilian immigrants who settled in New Orleans in the late 1800s. You'll find the elaborately constructed altars at local churches, including St. Louis Cathedral and the St. Joseph church on Tulane Avenue, as well as in Italian restaurants, community centers, and private homes. Of course, there's also a St. Joseph's Day Parade in the French Quarter. Why wouldn't there be?

ROLL ALONG
ON A FAMOUS NEW ORLEANS STREETCAR

The bright red or leafy green New Orleans streetcar is the iconic mode of getting around in the Crescent City. Traveling through the middle of major streets, such as St. Charles, Canal, Carrollton, and most recently North Rampart Street/St. Claude Avenue, the streetcar is an affordable ride that lets you watch the world go by with a clickety-clack soundtrack playing in the background. Tickets are just $1.25, but the experience, the timelessness of the rustic streetcar traveling down the track, is beyond measure. In a city loaded with historic references, the streetcar holds its own as the oldest continuously operating street railway system in the entire world, moving city-goers from place to place since the nineteenth century.

504-248-3900
norta.com

TIP

Buy a discounted Jazzy Pass,
(1-, 3-, and 31-day passes)
online and at ticket vending machines around
town and all Walgreens stores.

COUNT YOUR BLESSINGS
IN ST. ROCH CEMETERY

New Orleans is famous for its cemeteries, above-ground boneyards designed to keep the dead from literally washing away in this city built below sea level. One cemetery in particular whispers volumes to the imagination. Named for the twelfth-century French martyr, St. Roch Cemetery is a compact graveyard in the 7th Ward, a stroll from the restored St. Roch Market. Head past the monuments to the rear chapel, with its walls lined with ex-votos, offerings of thanks to St. Roch, along with leg braces, glass eyes, and even a pink plaster human heart. Handwritten notes, pictures of loved ones, and rusted crutches hang from the walls. While some tokens date back decades, some, such as a Post-it note bearing the hashtag "stay so very #alive," show that devotion is ongoing.

1725 St. Roch Ave.

SECOND LINE WITH MARDI GRAS INDIANS
ON SUPER SUNDAY

When it comes to mysterious New Orleans phenoms, Mardi Gras Indians top the list. Tracing their roots back to when Native Americans sheltered runaway slaves, the 50+ local tribes are known for spectacular hand-beaded and feathered costumes, call and response percussive music, and fierce pride in both neighborhood and tribe. Elusively present on Mardi Gras Day, the one day you can be sure to see them is Super Sunday, the Sunday closest to St. Joseph's Day (March 19). The brilliantly colored procession starts around noon at A.L. Davis Park (Washington and LaSalle Streets) in Central City, a dazzling only-in-New Orleans spectacle, where you'll see big chiefs in full regalia, entirely hand-sewn suits incorporating brightly colored plumes, beads, and glittering sequins and rhinestones into a dazzling panoply of folk art. Year-round, learn about Mardi Gras Indian culture at the Backstreet Cultural Museum and House of Dance & Feathers.

Backstreet Cultural Museum
1116 Henriette Delille St.,
504-577-6001
backstreetmuseum.org

House of Dance & Feathers
1317 Tupelo St.,
504-957-2678
houseofdanceandfeathers.org

SALUTE THE GREATEST GENERATION
AT THE NATIONAL WWII MUSEUM

Consistently ranked in the top 10 American museum experiences, the National World War II Museum delivers epic insights into the battles and everyday heroes of World War II. Located in New Orleans because it was home to Higgins Industries, the manufacturer of the landing craft that delivered U.S. troops onto the D-Day beaches, this CBD must-see will appeal to history lovers and anybody passionate about military lore. Interactive exhibits, including Campaigns of Courage: European and Pacific Theaters and the Road to Berlin, bring the people and places of World War II into sharp focus. For even more insight, reserve a spot at "Dinner with a Curator" at American Sector, a regular evening of historic conversation illuminated by chef Brooke Foster's inspired Southern comfort cuisine.

945 Magazine St., 504-529-1944
nationalww2museum.org

TIP
Have drinks at the American Sector,
the swell 1940s themed bar and restaurant adjacent to the museum.

945 Magazine St., 504-529-1940
nationalww2museum.org/american-sector/

TRACE SOUTHERN FOODWAYS
AND STIRRING COCKTAIL LORE

A pioneer of recent development in Central City, the Southern Food and Beverage Museum is a wondrous repository of the beloved Southern table. Housed in the former Dryades Street Market dating to 1849, the 16,000-square-foot space is dedicated to the food culture of fifteen Southern states and the District of Columbia and includes a wall devoted to the Museum of the American Cocktail. The realized vision of founder Liz Williams, a local dynamo with encyclopedic knowledge of food and cocktail history, SoFab offers ongoing cooking demonstrations in its Rouses Culinary Innovation Center by Jenn-Air and a slew of cool programs and exhibits. From celebrating Tujague's 160th birthday with colorful memorabilia to diving into the city's speakeasy past during Prohibition, SoFab dishes delicious perspective.

1504 Oretha Castle Haley Blvd., 504-267-7490
natfab.org/southern-food-and-beverage/

TIP
Make time during your visit to SoFab for nibbles and drinks at the adjacent Toup's South, the second restaurant from Cajun chef Isaac Toups of Bravo's *Top Chef* fame.

MIRE
ANTIQUES
2050

VEGAS
A MEN'S STORE

SHOPPING AND FASHION

TRY ON WIGS
AT FIFI'S

You won't know just how fab you'll feel in a cobalt pageboy until you try one on at Fifi Mahoney's on Royal Street. Home to towering pepto-pink bouffant wigs, glittery false eyelashes that put Tammy Faye to shame, and bright peacock feather headdresses, this place is a trip. Glamour pusses clamor for the outrageous theatrical makeup, spectacular wigs, and accessories geared to showstopping performances—drag and otherwise. Pay $5 for a stretchy hair sock, and try on wigs in every shade of the rainbow, an investment applied toward your purchase. Since you only live once, why not be fabulous every day and wear Fifi's whenever the mood strikes? That's quite OK in New Orleans, where pink hair is as common as Mardi Gras beads on the live oaks along St. Charles Avenue.

934 Royal St., 504-525-4343
fifimahonys.com

PERUSE A CENTURIES-OLD PUBLIC MARKET
BY THE RIVER

Wander down Esplanade toward the river on the quiet side of the French Quarter during the early morning and you'll run smack into the French Market as it's coming to life, a beehive of sellers unpacking their wares, artists setting up shop, and food vendors preparing all manner of delectables. The market was originally a Choctaw trading post dating back to 1791 and attracted French trappers, seafood hawkers, and more than a few rowdy sailors to its riverside hub. Today, one of the oldest farmers markets in America is open daily, a six-block open-air colonnade of produce, souvenirs, and freshly prepared local dishes, ranging from Gulf oysters to muffalettas. Besides the likes of alligator-on-a-stick and hot sauce, you'll find stands packed with jewelry, handbags, cheap sunglasses, and all things fleur-de-lys.

1235 N. Peters St., 504-596-3420
frenchmarket.org

TURN THE PAGE
AT AN INDIE BOOKSTORE

Independent bookstores may have gone the way of the dodo in other cities, but New Orleans's readers are a discriminating bunch. Here locally owned bookshops dish particular points of view, such as the warmly welcoming Kitchen Witch on Broad, specializing in all things cookery. On Frenchmen, Otis Fennel's FAB corner shop is beyond eclectic. At Faulkner House Books, rare books about the South, New Orleans, and Louisiana share space where William Faulkner once lived and wrote. Uptown, readers stay awhile at Maple Street Book Shop, a cozy spot full of interesting titles. Garden District Book Shop frequently spotlights local authors and runs an in-store book club open to all. At Tubby and Coos in Mid-City, a mash-up of used books, quirky special events, and themed book clubs add up to a novel experience.

FAB
600 Frenchmen St., 504-947-3700

Faulkner House Books
624 Pirate's Alley, 504-524-2940
faulknerhousebooks.com

Garden District Book Shop
2727 Prytania St., 504-895-2266
gardendistrictbookshop.com

Kitchen Witch Cookbooks
1452 N. Broad St., 504-528-8382
kwcookbooks.com

Maple Street Book Shop
7523 Maple St., 504-866-4916
maplestreetbookshop.com

Tubby and Coos
631 N. Carrollton Ave., 504-598-5536
tubbyandcoos.com

GET YOUR FEET
ON MAGAZINE STREET

Mall shopping has its fans and its place, but for a more personal retail experience at locally owned galleries and boutiques, Magazine Street is the avenue of dreams. A six-mile stretch that passes through the Garden District to Uptown, Magazine is heaven for fashionistas, nesters, and lovers of art and antiques. Along this anything but cookie-cutter array of shops, you can peruse vintage chic in colorful Victorian clapboards, pick out pillows in a columned Greek Revival home store, and ogle ornate imported Asian crafts and furnishings in a Creole cottage. Best of all, when you need to take a load off, dozens of inviting coffee shops, cafes, and bars are available to help you recharge.

504-342-4435
magazinestreet.com

EXPAND (OR START)
YOUR RECORD COLLECTION

You just can't download vinyl. Music purists in search of the retro hiss and pop of vintage LPs will find New Orleans a wealth of record emporiums showcasing both new and used vinyl. In the Marigny, the Louisiana Music Factory on Frenchmen Street is the go-to spot for local talent and all things jazz. Euclid Records in Bywater carries about 15 percent New Orleans artists, with an eclectic array making up the remainder of the 70,000 pieces of music, most of which are vinyl. Peaches Records on Magazine specializes in new vinyl in all genres, while Skully'z on Bourbon delivers everything from death metal to Motown new and used. In Mid-City, Domino Sound Shack preaches the gospel of reggae and world music along with local and indie releases.

Domino Sound Shack
2557 Bayou Rd., 504-309-0871
dominosoundrecords.com

Peaches Records
4318 Magazine St., 504-282-3322

Euclid Records
3301 Chartres St., 504-947-4348
euclidnola.com

Skully'z
907 Bourbon St., 504-592-4666
skullysrecords.com

The Louisiana Music Factory
421 Frenchmen St., 504-586-1094
louisianamusicfactory.com

PICK A PEKING DUCK
AT THE HONG KONG MARKET

It's less than ten miles from downtown to the Hong Kong Market on the West Bank in Gretna, but once you step into the massive supermarket, you might as well be halfway around the world. The newly expanded store has exotic Asian, Caribbean, and Latin ingredients for the adventurous home cook, along with well-priced produce and a great seafood department. This is the place to buy fragrant lemon grass, ginger, garlic and kaffir lime leaves, and then pick out a whole fish to stuff and cook on the grill. There's a busy meat department and a barbecue kiosk, where lacquered Peking ducks hang in clusters, and freshly roasted pig is carved into char siu and ribs. With oddball housewares, rice cookers, and a hundred kinds of rice, the riches in this global supermarket abound.

925 Behrman Hwy. #3, Gretna, 504-394-7075
hongkongmarketnola.com

BECOME SOMEONE ELSE
FOR A CHANGE

Playing dress-up isn't just for kids in New Orleans. Here, where costume shops are as common as family-owned grocery stores, you always have a reason and an opportunity to change your style. Whether for Halloween, Mardi Gras, or the Red Dress Run, you'll need all the essentials, such as a wig, sequins, a mask, and all manner of fantastical attire. Such stores as the New Orleans Party and Costume Shop and Southern Costume Company in the CBD are beyond comprehensive—jam-packed with wigs, hats, masks, glitter lashes, boas, and costumes of all ilk. In the Quarter, such funky spots as Le Garage on Decatur part the curtain on mind-bending sartorial treasures that will turn you into someone else altogether.

Le Garage Antiques & Clothing
1234 Decatur St.,
504-522-6639

Southern Costume Company
951 Lafayette St., 504-523-4333
sccnola.com

New Orleans Party & Costume
705 Camp St.,
504-525-4744

BUY ART
FROM THE PEOPLE WHO MAKE IT

Buy local isn't just about picking up a pound of PJ's coffee or selecting produce from a Louisiana farmer. New Orleans is a hotbed of artistic expression, a place where the boundaries and definition of art are always fluid. Support the local art community by buying, gifting, and collecting homegrown art. Sold at festivals and many indie neighborhood shops, local art is a fixture at ongoing markets in parks and reclaimed industrial spaces all over town. Palmer Park Art Market uptown is one of the biggest, a warren of textile, jewelry, sculpture, and painted inspiration across a swath of green space. Freret Market (also uptown), OCH Market in Central City, and the Art Garage on St. Claude Avenue are a few more options for bringing beauty into your world.

Freret Market
Freret St. and Napoleon Ave.,
504-638-2589
freretmarket.org

OCH Market
1618 Oretha C Haley Blvd.,
985-250-0278
ochartmarket.com

Art Garage
2231 St. Claude Ave.,
504-717-0750

BUY BITS OF HISTORY
ALONG ROYAL STREET

Crystal chandeliers, sword walking sticks, dazzling gems, ornate furniture, Confederate currency, and pop culture flotsam and jetsam from the mid-twentieth century are just a few of the treasures that await on Royal Street, one block off—but a world away from—raucous Bourbon Street. The city's oldest family-run antiques shops, with M.S. Rau at the top of the list, are clustered here, offering a bonanza of treasures to the avid antiquarian. Yes, you'll find the usual gorgeous nineteenth-century English and French furniture, rare stamps, and estate jewelry. Fittingly for New Orleans, though, a city of drinkers that positively drips with history, Lucullus Culinary Antiques is the spot for accoutrements for the ritualistic serving of absinthe, and rings with secret compartments for voodoo charms and poison turn up where you'd least expect.

M.S. Rau Antiques
630 Royal St., 888-557-2406
rauantiques.com

Lucullus Culinary Antiques
610 Chartres St., 504-528-9620
lucullusantiques.com

IMMERSE YOURSELF IN GLOBAL CULTURE
AT THE ALGIERS FLEA

Cross the bridge to the West Bank, and take the General McArthur exit, snaking back under the exit ramp to the base of the West Bank Expressway. If it's Saturday or Sunday, you're in for a multicultural shopping experience still undiscovered by most of the city's thrifterati and gourmands. Too bad for them, though, because this urban flea delivers a hodgepodge of used stuff, oddball crafts (goat-hoof jewelry?), and stalls selling delicious Central American and Mexican cuisine. Sample pupusas, thick cornmeal pancakes mixed with beans or cheese and served with pickled veggies and slaw. Take a break from dickering to tear into an outstanding carne asada or try costilla puerco—barbecued ribs slathered in a heavenly green sauce of onion, garlic, and tomatoes. This is cultural immersion of the tastiest kind.

105 Behrman Hwy., 504-361-1637

EAT YOUR WAY
THROUGH LOCAL MARKETS

For a city that loves to eat, there's been a dearth of local gourmet markets until the last few years—places to both eat and shop—such as the Reading Terminal in Philly and Granville Island Market in Vancouver. Redone after Katrina, the historic French Market isn't just about souvenirs and local art. There's also a revived focus on Louisiana growers, locally owned spots for nibbles, and a twice-weekly farmer's market. St. Roch Market reopened in 2014, selling both local produce and tasty dishes prepared by thirteen different vendors offering everything from oysters to Creole cuisine. Dryades Public Market transformed a former Central City school into a hybrid community market offering affordable staples, meat, and produce along with an oyster bar, sandwich counter, bakery, salad bar, and fresh pasta shop.

Dryades Public Market
1307 Oretha Castle Haley Blvd., 504-333-6100
dryadespublicmarket.com

French Market
1235 N. Peters St., 504-596-3420
frenchmarket.org

St. Roch Market
2381 St. Claude Ave., 504-609-3813
strochmarket.com

SUGGESTED
ITINERARIES

THE GREAT OUTDOORS

FEASTING AND COCKTAILING

NEAR THE NEW ORLEANS ERNEST N. MORIAL CONVENTION CENTER

ONLY IN NEW ORLEANS

GOOD FOR FAMILIES

DATE NIGHT

PARTY TIME

EATS ON THE CHEAP

Photo Credit: John Paris

ACTIVITIES
BY SEASON

While most New Orleans activities are year-round, the weather and calendar can also dictate what should top of your list.

SPRING

Super Sunday, 109

St. Joseph's Day, 105

Tennessee Williams/New Orleans Literary Festival, 57

Plantation Tours, 102–103

French Quarter Fest, 57

Jazz Fest, 60

Hogs for the Cause, 57

The Fly, 78

Destination Kitchen Food Tours, 44

New Orleans Wine & Food Experience, 31

SUMMER

Swamp Tour, 82

World War II Museum, 110

Historic New Orleans Collection, 99

City Park, 76

Rebirth at the Maple Leaf, 63

Satchmo Summerfest, 57

Tales of the Cocktail, 43

Southern Decadence, 92

• •